# *Chocolate*

# Chocolate

Audrey Tan

Marshall Cavendish
Cuisine

# Dedication

To my family, especially my nephew, Tay Woodward, who has been my inspiration behind some of these recipes.

# Acknowledgements

I thank the team at Saint Pierre for bearing with me and helping me out during the entire photography session. Special thanks go to Emmanuel and Edina for their support and understanding as we worked on this project. My appreciation also goes to the team at Marshall Cavendish Cuisine, namely David, Lydia and Lynn for working with me on the concept of this book and helping me make a dream come true. Thanks also to Joshua for his photography skills. And last but certainly not least, Hugo, Nann and Andrea for their time and infectious laughter.

The publisher wishes to thank Hugo, Nann and Andrea Petit for helping out with the photography of this cookbook.

Photographer : Joshua Tan, Little Black Box
Designer       : Lynn Chin Nyuk Ling
Recipe Writer : Cheva Yu

First published as Lust: For Love of Chocolate, 2005
This new edition 2009

Published by Marshall Cavendish Cuisine
An imprint of Marshall Cavendish International
1 New Industrial Road, Singapore 536196

Other Marshall Cavendish Offices:

Marshall Cavendish Ltd. 5th Floor, 32-38 Saffron Hill, London EC1N 8FH, UK • Marshall Cavendish Corporation. 99 White Plains Road, Tarrytown NY 10591-9001, USA • Marshall Cavendish International (Thailand) Co Ltd. 253 Asoke, 12th Flr, Sukhumvit 21 Road, Klongtoey Nua, Wattana, Bangkok 10110, Thailand • Marshall Cavendish (Malaysia) Sdn Bhd, Times Subang, Lot 46, Subang Hi-Tech Industrial Park, Batu Tiga, 40000 Shah Alam, Selangor Darul Ehsan, Malaysia

Marshall Cavendish is a trademark of Times Publishing Limited

National Library Board Singapore Cataloguing in Publication Data

Tan, Audrey, 1965-
Chocolate / Audrey Tan. – Singapore : Marshall Cavendish Cuisine, 2009.
p. cm.
ISBN-13 : 978-981-261-787-3
ISBN-10 : 981-261-787-6

1. Cookery (Chocolate)  2. Chocolate desserts.  I. Title.

TX767.C5
641.6374 -- dc22          OCN304017981

Printed in Singapore by Times Printers Pte Ltd

# Contents

# Foreword

Mention the word 'chocolate' and one can't help but feel yummy all over! The magical flavour that is chocolate is mystifying in its ability to hold mankind so captive to its lure. To me, a self-confessed chocoholic (thanks to my Belgian roots), it is as important as savoury food. I remember having to wait for a birthday or special occasion to enjoy what I considered as the pinnacle of gastronomy—my grandma's Flourless Belgian Chocolate Cake! In fact when I opened my first restaurant, she delivered the cakes every day rather than let me have the recipe! It was only when I moved overseas that she handed me her prized possession.

I met Audrey in Singapore when she had just returned from the States. Besides looking very cute (one of the reasons we hired her!), she gave us the impression that she was more than capable to handle our pastry section. We soon realised that Audrey was indeed a great asset to our team.

Audrey decided to remain grounded, after years of flying with a Hong Kong-based airline, and headed towards what she knew deep down she had always wanted to do. After completing her pastry course, she went under the tutelage of Pastry Chef Jeff Lehude of the Los Angeles Ritz Carlton. She joined Saint Pierre two years later and quickly became a favourite of all our customers, her colleagues (both kitchen and floor) and even our neighbours!

She was, initially, very classical in her presentation, but her infectious personality inevitably spilled over into her wonderful sweet creations, and they took on a unique style that is simply Audrey. As a pastry chef, Audrey is passionate about and partial to the uncomplicated. An analogy to her simple philosophy of baking is that a good chocolate mousse made from the best Belgian chocolate has nothing to hide, so it's best to be honest in the presentation by keeping it bare and simple!

Being privy to the progress towards her full potential fills me with great pride. In working on this book, Audrey has spent endless hours putting her recipes to paper and diligently tried them out on our team of happy guinea pigs…even the publishing team enjoyed the leftovers, and the shooting sessions became more of a long afternoon tea that lasted over a week!

Audrey's composition is simple and candid, and like chocolate, our "Mama" (as she is fondly regarded by her colleagues), is addictive and sweet.

*Emmanuel Stroobant*

*Enjoy the fruits of her labour!*

# Introduction

I was brought up by a nanny who was quite old, so by the time I was eight years old, we had our roles reversed. I had started to take charge of buying the groceries and running all the household errands that required a lot of legwork—and there began my love affair with chocolate! It was a treat that was readily available at the shops and did not cost too much for my old nanny to notice that some change was missing from the grocery purse!

Chocolate tastes so wonderful that 'sinful' and 'to die for' are the terms often used to describe it. As an ingredient, it conjures up such sweet and happy emotions, making it such a joy for me as I worked on sharing some of my favourite recipes in a cookbook for the first time. Working with chocolate is, for me, a pretty fail-proof way for preparing easy and tantalising sweets, which may be presented in various forms, such as cakes, puddings, mousse and soufflés.

The recipes in this cookbook are simply formulated and do not necessitate great talent for their success. Some of the more 'playful' recipes can also be handled by children without much difficulty. It is my hope that readers will find this book enjoyable and beneficial. My choice of these recipes has been based on their appeal to my imagined spectrum of readers and I trust I have deliberated with some degree of accuracy.

*Audrey Tan*

*Step into my sanctuary of chocolate delights!*

# Biscuits and Tarts

# White Chocolate Cookie Tarts

These tarts are very pretty especially with the piping.

| | |
|---|---|
| **White chocolate** | **200 g, chopped** |
| **Dark chocolate** | **50 g, chopped** |
| | |
| *Tart base* | |
| **Butter** | **120 g, softened** |
| **Sugar** | **80 g** |
| **Plain (all-purpose) flour** | **250 g, sifted** |
| | |
| *Filling* | |
| **Butter** | **90 g** |
| **Condensed milk** | **2 cans (each 397 g)** |

Prepare tart base. In a mixing bowl, beat butter and sugar until light and fluffy.

Add flour and knead lightly to form a dough. Be careful not to overwork ingredients.

Preheat oven to 180°C. Grease 20–24 tartlet tins.

Roll dough out between 2 sheets of baking paper to 0.5-cm thickness. Cut dough to fit tins and press into tins.

Bake for 15 minutes until dough is lightly brown. Leave dough to cool in tins.

For filling, place butter and condensed milk in a saucepan and stir over low heat until well combined, then remove from heat.

Return saucepan to stove and turn up heat to medium, stirring continuously for 10 minutes so mixture doesn't burn. Stir until mixture thickens. Pour mixture over cooled tart bases and leave to cool.

Melt white chocolate in a bain-marie and pour over cooled mixture on tart bases. Refrigerate for 1–2 hours.

Melt dark chocolate in a bain-marie and spoon into a piping bag. Pipe dark chocolate patterns over tarts as desired. Pop tarts out of tartlet tins before serving.

Makes 20–24 tarts

# Brownies

These brownies are extra delicious and moist with pecan nuts and sour cream. If you prefer your brownies to be even more moist, sandwich with a layer of chocolate ganache.

| | |
|---|---|
| **Butter** | **250 g** |
| **Dark chocolate** | **180 g, chopped** |
| **Large eggs** | **4** |
| **Sugar** | **500 g** |
| **Sour cream** | **120 g** |
| **Bread flour** | **180 g, sifted** |
| **Walnuts or pecan nuts** | **180 g** |
| **Chocolate ganache (optional) (see pg 135)** | |

Prepare brownies. Line a 20 x 20-cm baking tray. If using chocolate ganache, line 2 shallow 20 x 20-cm trays.

Melt butter and chocolate in a bain-marie.

In a mixing bowl, whisk eggs and sugar until ribbon-like in texture.

Add sour cream and whisk well. Add melted chocolate mixture and continue whisking.

Add flour and whisk on low speed for 10 minutes. Add nuts.

Preheat oven to 180°C.

Pour mixture into prepared baking tray or evenly into 2 shallow trays if using ganache.

Bake for 40–45 minutes if using 1 baking tray and 25–30 minutes if using 2 shallow trays.

Cool brownies in tray(s) and turn out after 20 minutes.

Meanwhile, make ganache if desired.

If serving plain, cut brownie into desired shapes before serving.

If serving with ganache, spread ganache over one layer of brownie with a spatula. Sandwich with other layer of brownie. Refrigerate for at least 30 minutes before serving.

Makes one 20 x 20-cm cake

# Sablé Biscuits

Nothing beats the taste of butter cookies covered with dark chocolate.

| | |
|---|---|
| **Butter** | **250 g, softened** |
| **Sugar** | **150 g** |
| **Cake flour** | **190 g, sifted** |
| **Bread flour** | **190 g, sifted** |
| **Vanilla bean** | **1, scraped for seeds, or 2 tsp pure vanilla essence** |
| **Dark chocolate** | **50 g, chopped** |

In a mixing bowl, combine all ingredients except dark chocolate and knead to form a dough.

Roll dough out onto a floured work surface and form a 6-cm long cylinder. Place dough on a small tray, cover with plastic wrap and chill in the refrigerator for 2–3 hours.

Preheat oven to 180°C.

Cut chilled dough into 1-cm thick discs and arrange on a lined baking tray, well spaced apart.

Bake for 20 minutes.

Remove biscuits from baking tray and cool on a wire rack.

Melt dark chocolate in a bain-marie. Temper chocolate, if desired.

Dip each biscuit halfway into melted chocolate, then place on a lined baking tray. Refrigerate for 5–10 minutes before serving.

Makes 24 biscuits

# Chocolate-Dipped Biscotti

Biscotti may take more time to make, but they are great snacks.

| | |
|---|---|
| **Sugar** | **180 g** |
| **Salt** | **a pinch** |
| **Cake flour** | **280 g, sifted** |
| **Baking powder** | **10 g, sifted** |
| **Almonds** | **125 g, chopped** |
| **Water** | **20 ml** |
| **Large eggs** | **2** |
| **Egg yolk** | **1** |
| **Dark chocolate** | **300 g, chopped** |

Combine sugar, salt, flour, baking powder and almonds in a mixing bowl.

In another bowl, combine water, eggs and egg yolk, then pour mixture into mixing bowl with dry ingredients to form a dough.

Using floured hands, work dough on a floured surface to form a flat disc. Place on a tray and cover with plastic wrap. Refrigerate for 1–2 hours.

Roll chilled dough out into a long flat roll, about 30 x 10 x 3-cm. Refrigerate for another 1 hour.

Preheat oven to 200°C.

Place chilled dough on a lined tray and bake for 20 minutes until evenly brown. Cool on a wire rack.

Slice dough thinly into 0.3-cm slices, on the diagonal, and place on a lined tray.

Lower oven temperature to 180°C and bake biscotti for another 10 minutes until dry and crisp.

Melt dark chocolate in a bain-marie. Dip each biscotti into melted chocolate and leave on a lined tray to set.

Serve or store in an airtight container.

Makes 20–30 biscotti slices

# Mini Chocolate Fruit Tartlets

These tiny, pretty fruit tartlets are a sure hit.

| | |
|---|---|
| **Pastry cream (see pg 140)** | |
| **Dark chocolate** | 200 g, chopped |
| **Fresh fruit** | |
| **Chopped pistachio nuts** | |
| | |
| *Tart dough* | |
| **Butter** | 125 g, softened |
| **Sugar** | 90 g |
| **Large egg** | 1, beaten |
| **Plain (all-purpose) flour** | 250 g, sifted |

Prepare tart dough. In a mixing bowl, beat butter, sugar and egg on low speed until well blended. If doing by hand, cream butter and sugar with a wooden spoon until light and fluffy, then add egg and mix well.

Add flour to form a dough. Flatten dough into a disc and cover with plastic wrap. Refrigerate for 30 minutes.

Grease and flour 15 small tartlet tins.

Preheat oven to 180°C.

On a floured work surface, roll dough out into a 0.3-cm thick sheet. Use a small round cutter to press out circles or use a knife to cut out small squares, depending on shape of tartlet tins.

Place dough into prepared tartlet tins, ensuring that dough is well pressed into sides and bottom of tins. Prick bottom of each tart with a fork.

Bake for 5–7 minutes until light golden. Leave to cool in tins.

Spoon pastry cream into a piping bag and pipe some cream onto base of tarts. Set aside.

Melt dark chocolate in a bain-marie.

Top each tart with melted chocolate. Invert tarts on a wire rack to let chocolate set.

Top with desired fruit and nuts to serve.

Makes about 15 tartlets

# White Chocolate Chip with Cashew Nut Cookies

*These cookies with soft centres are perfect with a glass of milk.*

| | |
|---|---|
| **Butter** | **110 g, softened** |
| **Brown sugar** | **100 g** |
| **Sugar** | **150 g** |
| **Large eggs** | **2** |
| **Honey** | **1 tsp** |
| **Bread flour** | **250 g, sifted** |
| **Baking soda** | **1 tsp, sifted** |
| **Cashew nuts** | **100 g, chopped and lightly roasted** |
| **White chocolate chips** | **100 g** |

In a mixing bowl, whisk butter and sugars until light and fluffy. Add eggs one at a time until well blended, then add honey.

Add bread flour, baking soda and nuts, then knead to form a dough.

On a floured work surface, roll dough out into a long cylinder about 5 cm in diameter. If dough is too moist to roll out, refrigerate for 1 hour before rolling.

Place shaped dough on a lined tray and cover with plastic wrap. Refrigerate for 2–3 hours.

Preheat oven to 170°C.

Cut chilled dough into 1-cm thick slices and arrange on a lined baking tray. Sprinkle chocolate chips over cookies, then bake for 15 minutes until golden brown.

Remove cookies from baking tray and cool on a wire rack before serving or storing in an airtight container.

*Makes about 25 cookies*

# Chocolate Raspberry Jam Cookies

An easy-to-do tea-time favourite.

**Raspberry jam**

**Chocolate ganache**
  **(see pg 135)**

*Cookies*

| | |
|---|---|
| **Butter** | 200 g, softened |
| **Sugar** | 150 g |
| **Large eggs** | 2 |
| **Plain (all-purpose) flour** | 260 g, sifted |
| **Ground almond powder** | 2 Tbsp |
| **Salt** | 1 tsp |

Prepare cookies. In a mixing bowl, beat butter and sugar until light and fluffy. Add eggs, one at a time until well blended.

Add flour, almond powder and salt and knead to form a dough. Roll dough into a ball and refrigerate for 1 hour.

Preheat oven to 180°C.

Roll chilled dough out into small balls each 2 cm in diameter. Use your thumb and press each ball of dough into the palm of your hand to a thickness of 1 cm (see small picture).

Arrange on a lined baking tray and bake for 18 minutes. Cool on a wire rack.

Pipe or spoon a drop of raspberry jam on each cookie, then pipe or spoon ganache over. Serve or store in an airtight container.

Makes about 24 cookies

# Chocolate Tarts with Citrus Fruits

A dark luscious treat, enough said.

| | |
|---|---|
| **Orange** | **1, peeled and segmented** |
| **Grapefruit** | **1, peeled and segmented** |
| | |
| *Sablé dough* | |
| **Butter** | **250 g, softened** |
| **Sugar** | **180 g** |
| **Large eggs** | **2, beaten** |
| **Plain (all-purpose) flour** | **500 g, sifted** |
| | |
| *Filling* | |
| **Milk** | **270 g** |
| **Egg yolks** | **2** |
| **Sugar** | **15 g** |
| **Dark chocolate** | **65 g, chopped** |

Preheat oven to 180°C. Grease and flour four 6-cm tartlet tins.

Prepare sablé dough. In a mixing bowl, beat butter, sugar and eggs on low speed until light and fluffy. Stir in flour to form a dough. Flatten dough into a disc and cover with plastic wrap. Refrigerate for 30 minutes.

On a floured work surface, roll chilled dough out to 0.3-cm thickness. Use a 9-cm round cutter to press out 4 tart circles.

Place dough circles into tartlet tins, ensuring that dough is well pressed into sides and bottom of tins. Prick bottom of each tart with a fork.

Bake until pale golden, about 8–10 minutes. Remove and leave to cool in tins.

Lower oven temperature to 160°C.

Prepare filling. In a saucepan, bring milk to the boil over medium heat. Use a cooking thermometer and keep watch. Once milk is 85°C, remove from heat immediately.

Meanwhile, beat egg yolks and sugar. Stir in some warm milk.

Pour mixture back into saucepan and return to heat, stirring continuously with a whisk. Add chocolate and stir well. Do not boil.

Remove tart shells from tins and place on a lined baking tray. Divide filling equally among tarts and fill to the rim of each shell.

Bake for 5–10 minutes until surface sets. Remove and cool on a wire rack.

Arrange orange and grapefruit segments on tarts. Serve immediately.

Makes four 6-cm tartlets

# Cakes, Breads and Puddings

# Tea Cakes

These irresistibly rich buttery tea cakes go well with a cup of hot tea.

| | |
|---|---|
| **Butter** | **250 g, softened** |
| **Sugar** | **250 g** |
| **Large eggs** | **5** |
| **Cream** | **250 ml** |
| **Plain (all-purpose) flour** | **320 g, sifted** |
| **Instant dried yeast** | **12 g** |
| **Chocolate** | **200 g, chopped** |
| **Chocolate ganache (optional) (see pg 135)** | |

Preheat oven to 165°C.

Grease muffin tins and line with paper muffin cups. Alternatively, place twelve 7-cm rings on a baking tray and line rings with baking paper cut to size.

In a mixing bowl, beat butter and sugar until light and fluffy. Add eggs, one at a time, until well blended.

Fold in cream, then fold in flour and yeast. Lightly fold in chopped chocolate.

Spoon about 3 Tbsp batter into muffin cups or pipe batter into prepared rings.

Bake for 20 minutes until risen and golden. To make sure cakes are properly cooked, insert a knife into the centres of cakes. The knife should come out clean.

Allow to cool for 2–3 minutes before turning onto a rack to cool.

When cakes are cool, top with chocolate ganache, if desired, before serving.

Makes 12 regular muffin-sized cakes

# Chocolate Fudge Cake

This is a drool-icious cake.

### Cake

| | |
|---|---|
| **Unsalted butter** | 225 g, softened |
| **Sugar** | 520 g |
| **Large eggs** | 3 |
| **Warm water** | 470 ml |
| **Cocoa powder** | 230 g, sifted |
| **Plain (all-purpose) flour** | 640 g, sifted |
| **Baking powder** | 10 g, sifted |
| **Baking soda** | 1 g, sifted |

### Fudge

| | |
|---|---|
| **Cream** | 240 ml |
| **Light corn syrup** | 120 ml |
| **Butter** | 30 g |
| **Milk chocolate** | 280 g, chopped |
| **Coffee liquor** | 50 ml |

Line a 20-cm round baking tin with baking paper or grease 24 cup cake tins. Preheat oven to 160°C.

In a mixing bowl, beat butter and sugar until light and fluffy, then add eggs, one at a time until well blended.

Mix in warm water gradually, then add cocoa powder, flour, baking powder and baking soda in batches, stirring well after each addition.

Pour batter into prepared tins and bake for 20 minutes.

Leave cake(s) to cool slightly, then refrigerate for 1 hour.

Prepare fudge. In a saucepan, combine cream, corn syrup and butter, and bring to the boil. Remove from heat and stir in milk chocolate, then liquor. If using immediately, whip fudge until stiff. Alternatively, refrigerate fudge for 2–3 hours, then whisk chilled fudge to soften it and increase its volume before using.

For a large cake, slice in half horizontally, then spread fudge on one layer of cake and sandwich with the other layer of cake. For cup cakes, simply spread fudge over top of cakes before serving.

Makes one 20-cm round cake or 24 small cup cakes

# Chocolate Cheesecake

A stunning cake with contrasting colours and textures.

| | |
|---|---|
| **Dark chocolate biscuits (Oreo)** | 380 g, cream scraped off, then crushed |
| **Butter** | 50 g, softened |
| **Honey** | 50 g |
| **Sour cream** | 100 g |
| **Cream cheese** | 600 g |
| **Sugar** | 100 g |
| **Lemon** | $^1/_2$, grated for zest |
| **Large eggs** | 4, beaten |
| **Chocolate ganache (see pg 135)** | |

Line base of a 20-cm round cake tin. Grease and flour sides of tin.

Preheat oven to 150°C.

In a mixing bowl, mix 300 g crushed biscuits, butter and honey until they resemble breadcrumbs. Press biscuit base into bottom of prepared tin.

In another mixing bowl, blend sour cream, cream cheese, sugar and lemon zest until smooth. Gradually add eggs until well mixed.

Fold in remaining crushed biscuits, then pour mixture over biscuit base.

Bake for 30 minutes until cake is set. Leave to cool in tin.

Pour chocolate ganache over cooled cheesecake in tin. Refrigerate for 4–5 hours, then unmould and serve.

Makes one 20-cm round cake

# Warm Dark Chocolate Cakes with Melting White Chocolate

This is a great twist on molten soft chocolate cakes. The secret lies in their white chocolate centres. Enjoy these cakes warm with vanilla ice cream.

| | |
|---|---|
| **Dark chocolate** | **500 g, chopped** |
| **Unsalted butter** | **500 g, melted** |
| **Sugar** | **350 g** |
| **Large eggs** | **10** |
| **Cake flour** | **400 g, sifted** |
| **Baking powder** | **30 g, sifted** |
| **White chocolate buttons** | **10** |

Preheat oven to 180°C. Set aside ten 8-cm ramekins or cake rings on a lined baking tray.

Melt dark chocolate and butter together in a bain-marie.

In a mixing bowl, beat sugar and eggs. Stir in melted chocolate-butter mixture.

Fold flour and baking powder, in 3 batches, into chocolate mixture.

Half-fill each ramekin or cake ring with chocolate batter.

Place a white chocolate button in the middle of each ramekin or cake ring. Fill over with more batter until each ramekin or ring is almost filled.

Bake for 12 minutes. Do not overbake.

The cakes will be very moist and their soft chocolate centres will flow out when sliced into.

Serve warm with vanilla ice cream, if desired.

Makes ten 8-cm cakes

# Chocolate Chip Milk Buns

These moist buns filled with chocolate are ideal for breakfast.

| | |
|---|---|
| **Milk** | **200 ml** |
| **Water** | **200 ml** |
| **Bread flour** | **500 g, sifted** |
| **Butter** | **20 g, softened** |
| **Sugar** | **20 g** |
| **Instant dried yeast** | **12 g** |
| **Dark chocolate chips** | **100 g** |

*Eggwash*

| | |
|---|---|
| **Egg yolks** | **2, beaten with a little water** |

Grease a baking tray.

Whisk milk and water and set aside.

In a mixing bowl with a dough hook, combine flour, butter, sugar and yeast using low speed.

Pour milk-water mixture in a slow, steady stream into mixing bowl and continue mixing at low speed for 8 minutes.

Increase to high speed and mix for another 8 minutes. A soft pliable dough should form. If ingredients are dry at this stage, add some milk or water to soften dough.

Cover mixing bowl with plastic wrap and leave to prove in a warm place for 1 hour until double in size.

Punch dough down, then divide into 50 g portions. Roll each portion into a ball with your palms.

Flatten each ball into a disc. Sprinkle 5–6 chocolate chips over and fold disc, then roll again into a perfect ball.

Place on prepared baking tray and brush with eggwash. Sprinkle more chocolate chips over.

Leave to prove for another hour until buns double in size.

Preheat oven to 180°C.

Bake for 20 minutes until light golden in colour. Buns should be light to the touch when lifted off tray.

Makes 20 small buns

# Dark Chocolate and Coconut Mousse Cake

This is a beautiful cake for the more adventurous baker. Use a 20-cm cake ring to assemble the cake. Follow the order of the recipe so both the chocolate and coconut mousse will be ready at the end just before assembling.

| | |
|---|---|
| **Dark chocolate shavings** | **100 g** |
| **Fresh fruit** | |
| | |
| *Genoise sponge cake* | |
| **Large eggs** | **4** |
| **Sugar** | **100 g** |
| **Plain (all-purpose) flour** | **100 g, sifted** |
| | |
| *Meringue* | |
| **Egg whites** | **6** |
| **Lemon juice** | **1 tsp** |
| **Sugar** | **280 g** |

*Genoise sponge cake*

Preheat oven to 180°C. Line a shallow baking tray (ensure that tray is larger than 20 cm) with baking paper.

In a mixing bowl, beat eggs and sugar until lighter in colour. Mix in flour a little at a time.

Pour batter into prepared tray and bake for about 12 minutes. To make sure cake is properly cooked, insert a knife into the centre of cake. The knife should come out clean.

Leave cake to cool in tray, then remove and peel off baking paper. Set aside.

*Meringue*

Preheat oven to 100°C. Draw a 20-cm circle on a piece of baking paper and place on a baking tray.

In a mixing bowl, beat egg whites on low speed. Add lemon juice and continue to beat until foamy.

Add one third of sugar and beat on high speed until soft peaks form. Gradually add remaining sugar and beat on high speed until meringue is firm and thick.

Spoon meringue into a piping bag and pipe onto circle drawn on baking paper. Start from centre of circle and move outwards until circle is filled.

Bake meringue for 1 hour, with oven door open until meringue disc hardens. It is fine if the centre of meringue disc is a little soft or moist. Allow to cool.

*Espresso*

Prepare espresso and sweeten to taste. Refrigerate.

*Espresso*

| | |
|---|---|
| **Espresso** | **125 ml** |
| **Sugar** | **to taste** |

*Chocolate mousse*

| | |
|---|---|
| **Gelatine sheets** | **2, softened in ice water** |
| **Dark chocolate** | **200 g, chopped** |
| **Large eggs** | **2** |
| **Egg yolks** | **4** |
| **Sugar** | **50 g** |
| **Water** | **3 Tbsp** |
| **Cream** | **380 ml** |

*Chocolate mousse*

Melt dark chocolate in a bain-marie. Set aside and allow to cool to room temperature.

In a medium bowl, beat eggs and egg yolks.

In a saucepan, heat sugar and water to 114°C for a syrup. Cook for 8–10 minutes.

Meanwhile, transfer beaten eggs to a mixing bowl and continue beating on low speed.

Once syrup is ready, pour in a steady stream into eggs while continuing to beat on low speed. Turn up speed to high and beat until mixture is light and pale. Set aside.

Warm a little cream in a bain-marie, then beat in softened gelatine sheets until well blended. Add remaining cream and beat until soft peaks form.

Fold in a quarter of whipped cream into cooled melted dark chocolate.

Fold in another quarter of whipped cream into whisked egg mixture, then fold in remaining whipped cream slowly.

Fold chocolate mixture into egg mixture. Refrigerate until ready to use.

*Coconut mousse*

| | |
|---|---|
| **Gelatine sheets** | **2, softened in ice water** |
| **Sugar** | **75 g** |
| **Coconut cream** | **185 ml** |
| **Cream** | **425 ml** |

*Coconut mousse*

In a saucepan, bring sugar and a third of coconut cream to the boil. Add softened gelatine sheets and stir well until dissolved.

Remove from heat and allow to cool for at least 30 minutes.

When mixtture is cool, add remaining coconut cream.

In another bowl, whip cream until soft to medium peaks form.

Fold whipped cream into cooled coconut cream mixture.

Refrigerate, covered with plastic wrap, until ready to use.

*Assembly*

Prepare a 20-cm cake ring and line a baking tray. Ensure that tray can fit in refrigerator.

Cut genoise sponge cake into an 18-cm circle and place on prepared baking tray. Brush with sweetened espresso until it is very moist.

Fit cake ring over cake.

Pour chocolate mousse over cake, letting it flow around sides of cake. Chill in the freezer for 30 minutes until lightly firm.

Place meringue disc over mousse and press gently downwards.

Pour coconut mousse over and smoothen top with a spatula. Refrigerate for 2 hours.

Use either a small blowtorch or a hot towel to unmould cake from cake ring.

Garnish with chocolate shavings and fresh fruit as desired.

Makes one 20-cm round cake

# Marble Cake

*This simple cake is always popular.*

| | |
|---|---|
| **Butter** | 360 g, softened |
| **Icing (confectioner's) sugar** | 360 g, sifted |
| **Large eggs** | 6, beaten |
| **Cake flour** | 100 g, sifted |
| **Baking powder** | 10 g, sifted |
| **Orange liquor** | 1 tsp |
| **Cocoa powder** | 8 g, sifted |
| **Milk** | 10 ml |

Grease and flour a 20 x 20-cm cake tin or 2 loaf tins.

Preheat oven to 220°C.

In a mixing bowl, beat butter and icing sugar until light and fluffy. Gradually add eggs until well blended.

Add flour and baking powder, then add orange liquor. Mix well.

Stir cocoa powder into milk. Transfer a third of cake batter to another bowl and add flavoured milk to thin it out.

Pour plain cake batter into prepared tin(s), then pour in cocoa-flavoured cake batter.

Bake for 15 minutes, then use a fork to make swirls in cake mixture.

Lower oven temperature to 180°C, then continue to bake for another 20 minutes. To make sure cake is properly cooked, insert a knife into the centre of cake. The knife should come out clean. Bake for another 5 minutes if necessary.

Remove cake from tin and cool on a wire rack before slicing to serve.

Makes one 20 x 20-cm cake or 2 loaves

# Chocolate Cake with White Chocolate Ganache

This is a luscious dark chocolate cake covered with a heavenly layer of white chocolate.

*Cake*

| | |
|---|---|
| **Butter** | **200 g, melted** |
| **Dark chocolate** | **220 g, chopped** |
| **Sugar** | **360 g** |
| **Hot water** | **125 ml** |
| **Large eggs** | **2, lightly beaten** |
| **Self-raising flour** | **200 g, sifted** |

*White chocolate ganache*

| | |
|---|---|
| **Cream** | **150 ml** |
| **White chocolate** | **400 g, chopped** |

Line a 20 x 20-cm square tin with baking paper.

Preheat oven to 160°C.

In a mixing bowl, combine butter, dark chocolate, sugar and hot water in a bain-marie.

Fold in beaten eggs, then flour. Pour batter into prepared tin and bake for 1 hour 30 minutes.

Meanwhile, prepare white chocolate ganache. In a saucepan, bring cream to the boil, then allow to cool.

Pour cooled cream slowly over chopped white chocolate while stirring. Refrigerate ganache for 30 minutes.

Unmould cake and pour ganache over. Spread ganache evenly over cake using a spatula, creating patterns on ganache as desired. Leave to set before slicing to serve.

Makes one 20 x 20-cm cake

# Chocolate Strawberry Shortcake

This is another popular tea-time favourite.

| | |
|---|---|
| **Strawberries** | **500 g (reserve 8 good whole ones for garnish), hulled and quartered** |
| **Almonds (optional)** | **500 g, sliced and lightly toasted** |
| *Cake* | |
| **Large eggs** | **6** |
| **Sugar** | **170 g** |
| **Salt** | **3 g** |
| **Cake flour** | **85 g, sifted** |
| **Corn flour (cornstarch)** | **50 g** |
| **Baking powder** | **1 g, sifted** |
| **Cocoa powder** | **25 g, sifted** |
| **Butter** | **70 g, softened** |
| *Cream* | |
| **Cream** | **1 litre** |
| **Icing (confectioner's) sugar** | **200 g, sifted** |

Preheat oven to 180°C. Grease and flour a 25-cm round cake tin.

Beat eggs, sugar and salt in a bain-marie until sugar and salt are dissolved.

Transfer to a mixing bowl and beat until light and fluffy.

Fold in cake flour, corn flour, baking powder and cocoa powder. Mix in butter.

Pour mixture into prepared cake tin and bake for 20 minutes. To make sure cake is properly cooked, insert a knife into the centre of cake. The knife should come out clean. Leave cake to cool in tin.

Prepare cream. Whip cream and icing sugar until stiff peaks form. Refrigerate until chilled, then spoon into a piping bag.

Remove cake from tin, then slice into halves horizontally.

Pipe a layer of cream on cake base.

Scatter quartered strawberries over cream, then sandwich with other cake layer.

Using a spatula, cover entire cake with cream. Press sliced almonds over sides of cake if desired. Decorate with remaining strawberries before serving.

Makes one 25-cm round cake

# White Chocolate Custard Cream Toasts

*A richer version of French toast for a special weekend breakfast.*

| | |
|---|---|
| **Pastry cream** | **500 g (see pg 140)** |
| **Cream** | **200 ml** |
| **White chocolate** | **180 g, chopped** |
| **White bread** | **8–12 slices, each 1-cm thick, crusts removed** |
| **Icing (confectioner's) sugar for dusting, sifted** | |
| **Mocha sauce or raspberry coulis (see pg 139)** | |
| **Fresh fruit** | |

Preheat oven to 250°C.

Line a baking tray with baking paper.

Leave pastry cream to soften in a bain-marie.

In a saucepan, bring cream to the boil. Pour over chocolate and stir well.

Fold chocolate mixture into softened pastry cream.

Dip each slice of bread into cream mixture and coat evenly. Place on prepared tray.

Bake for about 5–8 minutes until golden brown.

Dust toasts lightly with icing sugar, then arrange on a plate. Serve with mocha sauce or raspberry coulis and fresh fruit as desired.

Serves 4–6

# Chocolate Coffee Cake

This is a flavourful chocolate pound cake with a nuance of coffee.

| | |
|---|---|
| **Cocoa powder** | **50 g, sifted** |
| **Coffee** | **125 ml** |
| **Butter** | **120 g, softened** |
| **Sugar** | **250 g** |
| **Large eggs** | **3** |
| **Self-raising flour** | **200 g, sifted** |
| **Icing (confectioner's) sugar for dusting, sifted** | |

Grease and flour or line a 20-cm round cake tin.

Preheat oven to 180°C.

In a small bowl, slowly add sifted cocoa powder to coffee and stir into a paste.

In another bowl, beat butter and sugar until light and pale. Add eggs, one at a time and stir to blend well.

Fold in some flour and cocoa paste into batter, alternating the two until fully incorporated.

Pour batter into prepared tin and bake for 45 minutes. To make sure cake is properly cooked, insert a knife into the centre of cake. The knife should come out clean.

Leave cake to cool in tin for 20 minutes. Unmould and remove baking paper, if used.

Dust with icing sugar before serving.

Makes one 20-cm round cake

# Christmas Chocolate Fruit Cake

This is a cake to be ooh-ed and ahh-ed over at the Christmas table. Soaking the fruits in rum overnight and adding extra rum does even more wonders for this cake.

|  |  |
|---|---|
| **Raisins** | **750 g** |
| **Glacé cherries** | **250 g, chopped** |
| **Dried apricots** | **150 g, chopped** |
| **Orange juice** | **200 ml** |
| **Rum** | **125 ml** |
| **Dark chocolate** | **200 g, chopped** |
| **Butter** | **250 g, softened** |
| **Brown sugar** | **125 g** |
| **Large eggs** | **4** |
| **Apricot jam** | **125 g (or other jams of choice), at room temperature** |
| **Plain (all-purpose) flour** | **625 g, sifted** |
| **Ground nutmeg** | **$^1/_2$ tsp** |
| **White almonds** | **100 g, skinned and chopped** |
| **Extra rum (optional)** | |

In a large bowl, soak fruits in combined orange juice and rum mixture overnight.

Line a 23-cm round cake tin or 2 loaf tins with baking paper.

Preheat oven to 160°C.

Melt dark chocolate in a bain-marie.

In a mixing bowl, beat butter and brown sugar until light and fluffy. Stir in eggs, one at a time until well blended.

Add melted dark chocolate and jam gradually.

Add flour and ground nutmeg and stir to mix well.

Mix in fruits together with orange juice and rum mixture.

Pour mixture into prepared cake tin(s) and top with almonds. Bake for 2 hours 30 minutes to 3 hours. Unmould, peel off baking paper and cool on a wire rack.

Marinate by pouring more rum into cake, if desired.

Makes one 23-cm round cake or 2 loaves

# Hot Chocolate Pudding with Butterscotch Sauce

Just to savour the warm chocolatey and buttery goodness...

**Whipped cream**

*Pudding*

| | |
|---|---|
| **Butter** | **90 g, softened** |
| **Brown sugar** | **40 g** |
| **Large egg** | **1, beaten** |
| **Cream** | **100 ml** |
| **Plain (all-purpose) flour** | **110 g, sifted** |
| **Cocoa powder** | **4 Tbsp, sifted** |

*Butterscotch sauce*

| | |
|---|---|
| **Sugar** | **100 g** |
| **Butter** | **50 g** |
| **Cream** | **200 ml** |

Preheat oven to 180°C.

Grease 4 ramekins or ovenproof containers with 50 g softened butter.

In a bowl, beat remaining butter and brown sugar until light and fluffy. Mix in egg and cream until well blended.

Fold in flour and cocoa powder, then pour mixture into prepared ramekins. Bake for 20 minutes in a bain-marie.

Meanwhile, prepare butterscotch sauce. Caramelise sugar in a saucepan, then add butter. Pour cream in quickly, taking care as mixture will be hot and bubbly. Stir well with a wooden spoon until sauce is golden brown. Remove from heat.

Remove puddings from oven and immediately make a hole in each pudding with a teaspoon. Pour some sauce into holes, then serve warm with more butterscotch sauce and whipped cream.

Serves 4

# Chocolate Bread and Butter Pudding

A soft, warm comfort food which may be served in one large casserole or in a few small ramekins.

| | |
|---|---|
| **Milk** | **120 ml** |
| **Cream** | **500 ml** |
| **Sugar** | **100 g** |
| **Dark or milk chocolate** | **100 g, chopped** |
| **Butter** | **60 g, softened** |
| **Large eggs** | **4** |
| **Raisin bread** | **6 slices, each sliced into 4 triangles** |
| **Chocolate chips** | **100 g** |
| **Chocolate glaze (see pg 140)** | |
| **Milk or white chocolate shavings** | |

Preheat oven to 180°C.

Set aside a 20-cm casserole dish or some ramekins.

In a saucepan, bring milk, cream and sugar to the boil over medium heat. Add chopped chocolate and butter, then stir well for a silky finish.

Remove from heat and leave to cool for 10–15 minutes before stirring in eggs, one at a time.

Pour some mixture into a casserole dish or into ramekins.

Top with a layer of bread slices, then pour some more mixture over. Sprinkle some chocolate chips over.

Repeat layering once, then bake for 40–45 minutes until pudding sets and is golden brown.

Serve with chocolate glaze and garnish with milk or white chocolate shavings.

Makes one 20-cm pudding or several smaller puddings.

# Chocolate Beignets

These make a wonderful treat, served piping hot or warm with chocolate ice cream.

| | |
|---|---|
| Cocoa powder | 110 g, sifted |
| Large eggs | 4 |
| Sugar | 220 g |
| Vegetable oil | 55 ml |
| Milk | 230 ml |
| Bread flour | 400 g, sifted |
| Salt | a pinch |
| Dark chocolate | 100 g, chopped |
| Vegetable oil for deep-frying | |
| Icing (confectioner's) sugar for dusting, sifted | |
| Chopped pistachio nuts | |
| Chocolate ice cream (optional) (see pg 136) | |

Combine all ingredients, except dark chocolate, oil for frying, icing sugar and nuts, in a bowl.

Melt dark chocolate in a bain-marie and add to bowl. Stir well to form a dough.

Refrigerate dough for a few hours or overnight.

Remove chilled dough and divide into balls, each 5–6 cm in diameter.

Heat oil for deep-frying and deep-fry dough balls for a few minutes until they float.

Remove from oil and drain on absorbent paper.

Dust beignets with icing sugar and garnish with pistachios. Serve with chocolate ice cream (see pg 136) as desired.

Makes about 24 beignets

# Desserts

# Chocolate Liégeois

This should be made ahead of serving to allow for the frappe to freeze well.

| | |
|---|---|
| **Espresso** | **250 ml, sweetened** |
| **Cream** | **125 ml** |
| **Mascarpone** | **125 g** |
| **Sugar** | **40 g** |
| **Chocolate ice cream (see pg 136)** | |
| **Fresh fruit (optional)** | |
| **Icing (confectioner's) sugar for dusting, sifted** | |

| *Sponge fingers (optional)* | |
|---|---|
| **Egg yolks** | **5** |
| **Sugar** | **180 g** |
| **Egg whites** | **6** |
| **Plain (all-purpose) flour** | **115 g, sifted** |

To make frappe, pour espresso into a plastic tub and chill in the freezer for a few hours.

Prepare sponge fingers. Preheat oven to 180°C. Line a baking tray with baking paper.

Beat egg yolks with half the sugar until pale.

In a mixing bowl, whisk egg whites gradually with remaining sugar until stiff peaks form.

Fold egg white mixture into egg yolk mixture, then fold in flour. Spoon mixture into a piping bag and pipe 6-cm long fingers on prepared tray.

Bake for 5 minutes, then remove from oven for 5 minutes. Return fingers to oven and bake for another 5 minutes until golden brown. Set aside.

To make mascarpone cream, whip cream and mascarpone together, then stir in sugar.

Prepare some glasses.

Use a fork to scrape espresso frappe.

Spoon a layer of chocolate ice cream and mascarpone cream into glasses, then top with a layer of espresso frappe.

Chill in the freezer for 1 hour. Garnish with sponge fingers and fresh fruit as desired. Dust with icing sugar before serving.

Serves 6–8

# Chocolate Chip Walnut Muffins

*These muffins are deliciously moist and make a hearty snack anytime.*

| | |
|---|---|
| **Butter** | 110 g, softened |
| **Brown sugar** | 140 g |
| **Honey** | 100 g |
| **Large eggs** | 2, beaten |
| **Buttermilk or yoghurt** | 150 ml |
| **Walnuts** | 100 g, chopped |
| **Plain (all-purpose) flour** | 375 g, sifted |
| **Baking powder** | 6 g, sifted |
| **Baking soda** | 5 g, sifted |
| **Dark chocolate chips** | 300 g |

Grease 2–3 muffin trays. Alternatively, line a baking tray with baking paper and use 25 large paper muffin cups.

Preheat oven to 180°C.

In a mixing bowl, beat butter and sugar until light and fluffy. Stir in honey.

Fold in eggs, then fold in buttermilk or yoghurt.

Fold in walnuts, flour, baking powder and baking soda.

Fold in dark chocolate chips, reserving some for sprinkling over muffins.

Pour batter into muffin trays or paper muffin cups. Sprinkle remaining chocolate chips over if desired.

Bake for 25 minutes. When done, the surface of muffins will be springy when pressed lightly.

*Makes 12 large muffins*

# Chocolate Tiramisu

This popular favourite is both comforting and luxurious at the same time.

| | |
|---|---|
| **Sponge fingers** (see pg 71) | |
| **Chocolate ganache** (see pg 135) | |
| **Cocoa powder** for dusting, sifted | |

| *Tiramisu* | |
|---|---|
| **Cocoa powder** | 1 Tbsp |
| **Coffee liquor** | to taste |
| **Coffee** | 500 ml |
| **Large eggs** | 6, whites and yolks separated |
| **Icing (confectioner's) sugar** | 200 g, sifted |
| **Cream** | 250 ml |
| **Mascarpone** | 250 g |

Prepare tiramisu. In a bowl, combine cocoa powder, coffee liquor and coffee and mix well. Set aside.

In another bowl, beat egg yolks and half the icing sugar until light and fluffy.

In a third bowl, beat egg whites and remaining icing sugar until medium to stiff peaks form.

In a fourth bowl, beat cream until soft peaks form.

Fold egg yolk mixture into egg white mixture, then fold in cream and mascarpone.

To assemble tiramisu, place sponge fingers in cocoa-coffee mixture until thoroughly soaked.

Pack a layer of soaked sponge fingers tightly at the base of a casserole dish. Alternatively, used several smaller cups or glasses.

Spoon a layer of egg-mascarpone mixture over soaked sponge fingers, then top with a layer of chocolate ganache.

Repeat layering and finish with egg-mascarpone mixture layer on top.

Refrigerate for 4–5 hours for flavours to develop.

Dust well with cocoa powder before serving. Decorate as desired.

Makes a 20-cm cake or several smaller cakes

# Chocolate Panna Cotta with Mango and Fresh Mint

*Serve this in clear glasses for a light and colourful dessert.*

| | |
|---|---|
| **Cream** | **500 ml** |
| **Brown sugar** | **50 g** |
| **Vanilla bean** | **1, scraped for seeds and reserve pod, or 1 tsp pure vanilla essence** |
| **Gelatine sheets** | **3, softened in ice water** |
| **Chocolate glaze (see pg 140)** | |
| **Mango slices** | |
| **Mint leaves** | |
| **Icing (confectioner's) sugar for dusting, sifted** | |

In a saucepan, bring cream to the boil with brown sugar and vanilla seeds and pod. Leave to cool for 30 minutes, then strain.

Add gelatine sheets and stir well.

Refrigerate for at least 30 minutes before pouring into several martini or cocktail glasses. Refrigerate overnight until panna cotta is lightly set.

Drizzle chocolate glaze over panna cotta and garnish with sliced mango and mint leaves. Dust with icing sugar as desired.

*Makes 8–10 small glasses*

# Banana Delight

*This is banana split reinvented with dark chocolate and presented in an even more fun way.*

| | |
|---|---|
| **Dark chocolate** | 500 g, chopped |
| **Large bananas** | 6 |
| **Roasted almonds** | 100 g, chopped |

Line a baking tray with baking paper.

Peel bananas and spear each one with a thin bamboo skewer or fork.

Melt dark chocolate in a bain-marie.

Dip each banana into melted chocolate and coat completely.

Scatter chopped almonds over one end of each coated banana. Place on prepared tray.

Refrigerate, uncovered, for 1 hour before serving.

# French Crêpes with Chocolate and Sautéed Apples

*Popularly eaten for breakfast or dessert.*

**Chocolate mayonnaise**
  **(optional) (see pg 135)**

**Chocolate glaze**
  **(optional) (see pg 140)**

*Crêpes*

| | |
|---|---|
| **Plain (all-purpose) flour** | 340 g, sifted |
| **Sugar** | 85 g |
| **Salt** | 2 tsp |
| **Large eggs** | 6, beaten |
| **Egg yolks** | 6, beaten |
| **Butter** | 170 g, melted |
| **Milk** | 660 ml |
| **Orange** | 1, finely grated for zest |

*Apples*

| | |
|---|---|
| **Sugar** | 50 g |
| **Butter** | 20 g |
| **Apples** | 3, peeled, cored and quartered |

Prepare crêpes. Combine flour, sugar and salt into a bowl. Add eggs and egg yolks, then butter, milk and orange zest. Stir well. The batter will be smooth and a little runny. Add more milk to thin batter if it is too thick.

Heat an 18-cm non-stick pan over low heat.

Ladle a scoop of batter into pan.

Brown one side of crêpe before flipping over to brown other side. Repeat until batter is used up. Set crêpes aside.

Prepare apples. In a saucepan, caramelise sugar. Add butter and sauté apples until golden brown.

Serve crêpes with sautéed apples and your choice of chocolate mayonnaise or chocolate glaze. Sprinkle sugar crystals over before serving, if desired.

Serves 4–6

# White Chocolate Parfait with Dark Cherries

This is a cold creamy dessert with divine colours.

| | |
|---|---|
| **White chocolate** | **300 g, chopped** |
| **Eggs** | **4, whites and yolks separated** |
| **Cream** | **500 ml** |
| **Dark cherries** | **400 g, pitted and halved** |
| **Brown sugar** | **25 g** |

Line a loaf tin or any desired mould with baking paper, overlapping the edges.

Melt white chocolate in a bain-marie.

In a mixing bowl, whisk egg yolks and a third of cream until soft peaks form.

In another bowl, whisk egg whites with another third of cream until stiff peaks form.

In a third bowl, whisk remaining cream until stiff peaks form. Fold cream into egg yolk mixture, then fold in melted white chocolate. Fold in egg white mixture.

Pour half the mixture into prepared tin.

Spoon 150 g cherries in the middle of parfait mixture.

Pour remaining mixture over cherries.

Chill in freezer for 3–4 hours until parfait is set.

Sauté remaining cherries with brown sugar until juices run. Remove from heat before cherries turn too soft. Leave to cool.

Remove parfait from freezer and lift baking paper to unmould.

Slice parfait, arrange on a plate and serve with sautéed cherries.

Serves 6–8

# Chocolate Coffee Crème Brûlée

Tastes simply wonderful and doesn't require a lot of time to do. Serve in ramekins or coffee cups for a different effect.

| | |
|---|---|
| **Cream** | **400 ml** |
| **Dark chocolate** | **100 g, chopped** |
| **Egg yolks** | **5, beaten** |
| **Sugar** | **70 g** |
| **Instant coffee powder** | **1 Tbsp** |
| **Milk** | **100 ml** |
| **Extra sugar to caramelise (optional)** | |

Preheat oven to 130°C.

In a saucepan, bring cream to the boil. Add dark chocolate and stir well.

In a bowl, beat egg yolks and sugar. Stir in some warm chocolate-cream mixture to temper egg yolks.

Pour tempered mixture back into saucepan and mix well with remaining chocolate-cream mixture.

Dissolve coffee powder in milk and add to saucepan.

Half-fill 4 ramekins or coffee cups with mixture. Place in a bain-marie and bake for 40–45 minutes.

Leave to cool slightly, then refrigerate for 2–3 hours. Sprinkle with sugar and caramelise lightly with a blowtorch, if desired.

Serve plain or topped with whipped cream.

Serves 4

# Chocolate Mini Pots

This is wonderful served in small glasses or ramekins.

| | |
|---|---|
| **Milk** | **1 litre** |
| **Cocoa powder** | **40 g** |
| **Egg yolks** | **10** |
| **Sugar** | **200 g** |
| **Fresh fruit (optional)** | |

Preheat oven to 150°C.

Set aside 6–8 ovenproof glasses or ramekins.

In a saucepan, bring milk and cocoa powder to a simmering boil, then remove from heat.

In a bowl, beat egg yolks and sugar. Stir in some warm cocoa-milk mixture to temper egg yolks.

Pour tempered mixture back into saucepan and mix well. Stir over low heat.

Pour mixture into glasses or ramekins. Place in a bain-marie and bake for 35 minutes.

Serve plain or with fresh fruit as desired.

Serves 6-8

*Photo on pg 86–87*

# Millefeuille of Caramelised Banana, Wonton Skins and Chocolate Glaze

This is delicious and it has many different textures to tickle the taste buds. Use Del Monte bananas and Tia Maria for the best results.

| | |
|---|---|
| **Sugar** | **80 g** |
| **Butter** | **50 g** |
| **Large bananas** | **8, peeled and sliced** |
| **Coffee liquor (optional)** | |
| **Vegetable oil for deep-frying** | |
| **Wonton skins** | **12** |
| **Icing (confectioner's) sugar for dusting, sifted** | |
| **Chocolate glaze (see pg 140)** | |

Over medium heat, caramelise sugar until golden. Add butter and stir well.

Add banana slices and coat evenly with caramel.

Flambé with coffee liquor as desired. Set aside to cool.

Heat oil for deep-frying and deep-fry wonton skins until light golden and bubbly in texture. Drain well and set aside.

Arrange banana slices and wonton skins on serving plates.

Dust lightly with icing sugar and drizzle chocolate glaze over before serving.

Serves 6

# Chocolate Soufflé

These soufflés take almost no time to assemble and they are impressive when done well. Use ramekins with straight lips so that the soufflés will rise.

| | |
|---|---|
| **Butter** | **50 g, softened** |
| **Sugar for coating ramekins** | |
| **Pastry cream** | **250 g (see pg 140)** |
| **Cocoa powder** | **50 g, sifted** |
| **Egg whites** | **8** |
| **Sugar** | **50 g** |
| **Icing (confectioner's) sugar for dusting, sifted** | |
| **Rasberry coulis (optional) (see pg 139)** | |

Preheat oven to 180°C.

Grease four 8-cm ramekins with softened butter.

Pour sugar into a ramekin, then tilt to coat interior evenly. Tap lightly and pour into next ramekin. Repeat until all 4 ramekins are coated evenly with sugar. Discard excess sugar used for coating ramekins.

Soften pastry cream in a bain-marie for 5–10 minutes. Add cocoa powder and whisk well.

Beat egg whites until foamy. Add sugar gradually while continuing to whisk until stiff peaks form.

Fold egg whites in 3 batches into whisked cocoa-pastry cream. Pour mixture into ramekins.

Use the tip of a small knife to run around the edge of the soufflé batter in each ramekin, then bake for 10 minutes.

Dust with icing sugar and serve immediately with raspberry coulis and vanilla ice cream, if desired.

Makes four 8-cm soufflés

# Chocolate Flan

This chocolate flan is easy and fun to make as well as to eat! Instead of using a large flan pan, use small containers so that the caramel and flan layers are easily visible when cut into.

**Whipped cream**
  **(optional)**

**Fresh fruit**
  **(optional)**

*Caramel*

| | |
|---|---|
| **Water** | 200 ml |
| **Sugar** | 200 g |

*Custard*

| | |
|---|---|
| **Cream** | 185 ml |
| **Milk** | 500 ml |
| **Large eggs** | 4, beaten |
| **Sugar** | 45 g |
| **Dark chocolate** | 200 g, chopped |

Preheat oven to 150°C.

Set aside a flan pan or 8 small ovenproof glasses or cups.

Prepare caramel. In a saucepan, bring water and sugar to the boil over medium heat until golden brown. Remove from heat. Do not let caramel turn too dark or it will taste bitter.

Pour caramel immediately into flan pan or divide equally among cups. Tilt flan pan or cups to coat bottom(s) evenly. Let caramel set.

Prepare custard. In a saucepan, bring cream and milk to the boil.

In a bowl, beat eggs and sugar until soft peaks form. Stir in some hot cream.

Pour mixture back into saucepan and mix well with remaining cream mixture. Bring to a gentle boil, then add dark chocolate and stir well.

Pour mixture into flan pan, glasses or cups. Bake for 40–45 minutes. Allow to cool in pan, glasses or cups.

Use the tip of a small knife to run around the edges of flan. Cover pan or each cup with a high-rimmed plate and flip over quickly. The flan should pop out neatly onto plate.

Serve with whipped cream and fresh fruit as desired.

Makes one 20-cm flan or several smaller flans

# Poached Pears with Pink Peppercorns and White Chocolate Cream Sauce

A sensuous and smooth dessert. Choose hard green pears for poaching and use green peppercorns if pink peppercorns are unavailable. Do not use black peppercorns as they are too harsh for this recipe.

| | |
|---|---|
| **Green pears** | **4, peeled** |
| **Sugar** | **450 g** |
| **Water** | **1.5 litres or enough to cover pears in saucepan** |
| **Pink peppercorns (optional)** | **5** |
| **Vanilla bean (optional)** | **1, scraped for seeds and reserve pod** |
| **Pastry cream** | **150 g (see pg 140)** |
| **White chocolate** | **70 g, chopped** |
| **Cream** | **300 ml** |
| **Chocolate glaze (see pg 140)** | |

Place pears and sugar in a heavy-based saucepan and cover with enough water. Heat, stirring to dissolve sugar. Add peppercorns and/or vanilla seeds and pod and bring to the boil.

Lower hear and simmer for 1 hour 30 minutes to 2 hours until pears are cooked through. Test with the tip of a knife. The knife should go cleanly into pears. If not, simmer for a few minutes more.

In a mixing bowl, soften pastry cream on low speed for 2–3 minutes, or use a hand whisk.

Place pastry cream in a bain-marie for a few minutes to heat, then add white chocolate and stir well to blend.

Whip cream lightly, then fold into white chocolate mixture.

Cut each pear in half vertically and core. Fill hollowed-out cores with white chocolate cream sauce or chocolate glaze. Drizzle with more chocolate glaze to serve.

Serves 4

# Chocolate Trifle with Mixed Berries

This appealing trifle comes with many colours and textures.

**Genoise sponge cake**
  **(see pg 47) or**
  **Sponge fingers**
  **(see pg 71)**

**Mocha sauce**
  **(see pg 139)**

**Mixed berries**

**Icing (confectioner's)**
  **sugar for dusting,**
  **sifted**

*Mousse*

| | |
|---|---|
| **Butter** | 120 g, softened |
| **White chocolate** | 200 g, chopped |
| **Egg yolks** | 4 |
| **Sugar** | 100 g |
| **Espresso powder** | 2 Tbsp |
| **Cream** | 150 g |

Prepare a medium-sized glass bowl or 6–8 glasses.

Prepare sponge cake or sponge fingers.

Prepare mousse. Melt butter and chocolate in a bain-marie. Beat egg yolks and sugar until light and fluffy. Stir in espresso powder. Combine butter-chocolate mixture with egg yolk mixture. Whip cream until soft peaks form, then fold into combined mixture.

Spoon a layer of mousse into prepared glass bowl or glasses. Add some mixed berries, then top with a layer of sponge cake or sponge fingers. Layer with mocha sauce, mousse and mixed berries.

Refrigerate for 2–3 hours. Dust with icing sugar as desired before serving.

Serves 6–8

# Petits Fours

# Chocolate-Dipped Pâte Cigarettes

*These elegant petits fours take their name from their shape.*

| | |
|---|---|
| **Egg whites** | 2 |
| **Sugar** | 120 g |
| **Plain (all-purpose) flour** | 4 Tbsp, sifted |
| **Butter** | 60 g, softened |
| **Preferred chocolate** | 200 g, chopped |
| **Pistachio nuts or other nuts** | 100 g, chopped |

Preheat oven to 180°C.

Line a baking tray with baking paper or use a silpat mat.

Mix egg whites, sugar, flour and butter into a paste.

Using 2 fingers, smooth paste into 6-cm wide circles on prepared tray or silpat mat. Bake 5 circles at a time.

Bake for 10 minutes and ensure that circles are not too dark.

Once out of the oven, roll circles into cigarettes. If circles become too hard to roll, warm briefly in oven before rolling again.

Melt chocolate in a bain-marie.

Dip one or both ends of each cigarette in melted chocolate. Roll over nuts, then leave to set.

*Makes about 18 cigarettes*

# Chocolate Coconut Squares

These are incredibly easy to make and fun to eat.

| | |
|---|---|
| **Chocolate rice puffs** | **125 g** |
| **Brown sugar** | **60 g** |
| **Self-raising flour** | **60 g, sifted** |
| **Cocoa powder** | **1 Tbsp, sifted** |
| **Large egg** | **1, lightly beaten** |
| **Desiccated coconut** | **2 Tbsp + extra for coating** |
| **Butter** | **125 g, melted** |

Preheat oven to 180°C.

Line a 20 x 20-cm baking tin with baking paper.

Crush rice puffs in a plastic bag with a rolling pin or a heavy object. Alternatively, place them in a blender to get fine crumbs.

In a large bowl, combine brown sugar, flour, cocoa powder and crushed rice puffs. Stir in egg, desiccated coconut and lastly, butter. Mix well.

Transfer mixture into prepared tray and bake for 20 minutes. Remove from oven and leave to cool in tray.

Cut into squares and coat with extra desiccated coconut before serving or storing.

Makes about 20 squares

# Chocolate Lollipops with Rice Puffs

This is a chocolate treat everyone will love. Lollipop sticks are available from baking supplies shops. Alternatively, use cocktail forks.

| | |
|---|---|
| **Cream** | **120 ml** |
| **Dark chocolate** | **200 g, chopped** |
| **Honey** | **2 Tbsp** |
| **Chocolate rice puffs** | |

In a saucepan, bring cream to the boil.

Place dark chocolate and honey in a bowl.

Remove cream from heat and pour over dark chocolate and honey. Stir to mix well. Refrigerate for 1 hour.

Using gloves, roll chocolate mixture into balls, each 3–4 cm in diameter.

Place chocolate rice puffs on a flat dish and roll each chocolate ball over to coat evenly.

Attach each ball to a lollipop stick or cocktail fork. Alternatively, use small paper cups if sticks or forks are not available.

Serve or store in a cool place.

Makes 20–25 lollipops

# Financiers

These traditional French petits fours are fragrant and wonderful with a cup of tea.

| | |
|---|---|
| **Butter** | 250 g, melted |
| **Ground almond powder** | 250 g |
| **Cake flour** | 125 g, sifted |
| **Icing (confectioner's) sugar** | 500 g, sifted |
| **Egg whites** | 10 |
| **Whole vanilla bean** | 1, scraped for seeds, or 2 tsp pure vanilla essence |
| **Dark chocolate chips** | 24 |

Preheat oven to 180°C.

Lightly grease twenty-four 6 x 2-cm cake moulds or small foil cups.

In a mixing bowl, combine all ingredients, except dark chocolate chips.

Refrigerate for 3 hours, covered with plastic wrap, until mixture is slightly firmer.

Spoon mixture into a piping bag and pipe into tins or cups.

Press a chocolate chip into each portion of batter.

Bake for 15 minutes. Remove from oven and leave to cool in tins or cups.

Makes 24 financiers

# White Chocolate Truffles

These luxurious treats are surprisingly easy to make.

| | |
|---|---|
| **Cream** | **120 ml** |
| **Dark chocolate** | **200 g, chopped** |
| **Ground cinnamon** | **$^1/_2$ tsp** |
| **White chocolate** | **200 g, chopped** |
| **Milk chocolate** | **100 g, chopped** |

Line 2 baking trays with baking paper.

In a saucepan, bring cream to the boil. Add dark chocolate and stir to blend well. Add ground cinnamon.

Refrigerate for a few hours, covered with plastic wrap, until chocolate mixture is firm.

Using plastic gloves, roll mixture into balls, each 3 cm in diameter. Set on a lined tray.

Temper white chocolate (see pg 143).

Dip each truffle in white chocolate using a fork or stick. Ensure that truffles are well coated. Set truffles on other lined tray.

Melt milk chocolate in a bain-marie and spoon into a piping bag. Decorate truffles with milk chocolate streaks.

Chill well before serving.

Makes about 25 truffles

# Mini Chocolate Pavlova Meringues

*These meringues are a treat at any time of the day.*

| | |
|---|---|
| **Egg whites** | **6** |
| **Sugar** | **300 g** |
| **Corn flour (cornstarch)** | **30 g** |
| **Dark chocolate chips** | **150 g** |

Preheat oven to 180°C.

Line a baking tray with baking paper and arrange 30 mini paper cups on tray.

In a mixing bowl, beat egg whites until foamy. Continue to beat egg whites, adding 280 g sugar gradually. Beat until stiff peaks form.

Lower speed and add corn flour and remaining sugar.

Increase speed and beat until stiff peaks form. The mixture should be firm and glossy.

Spoon or pipe mixture into mini paper cups. Fill paper cups up halfway.

Add a few dark chocolate chips to each cup, then spoon or pipe over with more meringue. Bake for 1 hour until meringues are light and dry.

Leave to cool before serving or storing in an airtight container.

Makes 30 meringues

*Photo on pg 111*

# Chocolate Marshmallow Cakes

*This is a definite hit with the kids, especially the big ones.*

| | |
|---|---|
| **Ginger snap cookies** | **200 g** |
| **White chocolate** | **100 g, chopped** |
| **Dark chocolate** | **300 g, chopped** |
| **White mini marshmallows** | **200 g** |
| **Walnuts** | **150 g, chopped** |
| **Yellow raisins** | **90 g** |

Crush cookies in a plastic bag with a rolling pin or a heavy object. Alternatively place them in a food processor (blender) to get fine crumbs.

Melt white chocolate in a bain-marie and add crushed cookies.

Press white chocolate biscuit mixture into a greased or lined flat, rectangular tray. Alternatively use cup cake moulds.

Melt dark chocolate in a bain-marie and stir in marshmallows, walnuts and raisins.

Pour dark chocolate mixture over crushed cookie layer and press down gently with a wooden spoon.

Refrigerate for 2 hours until set. Cut to serve.

Serves 6–8

# Chocolate Fruit and Nut Candy

This is a perfectly scrumptious holiday snack.

| Icing (confectioner's) sugar | 500 g, sifted |
|---|---|
| Evaporated milk | 350 ml |
| Butter | 45 g |
| Dark chocolate | 175 g, chopped |
| Assorted nuts | 100 g, chopped |
| Raisins | 30 g |
| Dried apricots | 55 g |
| White chocolate | 400 g, chopped |

In a saucepan, bring icing sugar, evaporated milk and butter to the boil for 8–10 minutes at 115°C. Use a cooking thermometer to monitor temperature.

Transfer to a mixing bowl. Add dark chocolate and beat until colour changes to a lighter tone. Add nuts and fruit.

Pour mixture into a deep 20 x 20-cm pan and refrigerate for 1–2 hours.

Turn candy out of pan and cut into squares with an oiled knife. Re-shape with gloved fingers. Attach candy squares to ice cream sticks or cocktail forks as desired.

Melt white chocolate in a bain-marie.

Dip candy squares in melted white chocolate and leave to set before serving or storing.

Makes one 20 x 20-cm square block

# White Chocolate Clusters

These tiny gems are delightful as a light snack at any time of the day.

| | |
|---|---|
| **White chocolate** | **300 g, chopped** |
| **Dried apricots** | **50 g, diced** |
| **Dried cranberries** | **50 g, diced** |
| **Pistachio nuts** | **50 g, diced** |
| **Walnuts** | **50 g, diced** |

Line a baking tray with baking paper.

Temper white chocolate (see pg 143). Cool chocolate to room temperature.

Spoon cooled chocolate into a piping bag and pipe chocolate drops, each 2-cm in diameter, onto prepared tray.

Press a small handful of fruit and nuts into each chocolate drop. Leave to set.

Serve or store in the refrigerator.

Makes 25–30 chocolate clusters

# Profiteroles with Chocolate Sauce

These little choux puffs are filled with pastry cream and topped with dark chocolate. They may take a few more steps to prepare, but are definitely worth the effort.

**Pastry cream
   (see pg 140)**

*Choux pastry*

| | |
|---|---|
| **Water** | **250 ml** |
| **Salt** | **10 g** |
| **Butter** | **140 g, cold, cut into cubes** |
| **Plain (all-purpose) flour** | **150 g, sifted** |
| **Large eggs** | **3** |

*Chocolate sauce*

| | |
|---|---|
| **Milk** | **100 ml** |
| **Dark chocolate** | **180 g, chopped** |

Preheat oven to 180°C. Line a baking tray with baking paper.

Prepare choux pastry. In a saucepan, bring water, salt and butter to a gentle boil.

Lower heat and add flour all at once. Stir well with a wooden spoon until dough pulls away from sides of saucepan and forms a dough.

Remove from heat and transfer dough to a mixing bowl. Add 1 egg at a time into dough and mix well after each addition. Make sure that eggs are well blended into dough. The dough will be smooth, moist and a little stiff. To test, raise dough surface with the back of the wooden spoon to form a peak. The dough should hold its shape.

Spoon dough into a piping bag and pipe 2.5-cm balls well spaced apart onto prepared tray.

Bake for 10 minutes until dry. Do not open oven door. Leave puffs to continue cooking in heat. When done, puffs will be light. Set aside.

Prepare chocolate sauce. In a saucepan, bring milk to the boil and add chocolate. Stir well until chocolate is melted.

Make a hole in the base of each profiterole with a chopstick. Alternatively, slice each profiterole in half horizontally.

Spoon pastry cream into a piping bag and pipe into profiteroles. Dip filled profiteroles in chocolate sauce and leave to set before serving.

Makes about 24 profiteroles

# Almond Chocolate Tuiles

Tuiles are magnificent and beautiful as a garnish. They are also easy and quick to make. For ease of handling, use a silpat mat, available from baking supplies stores. The tuiles will peel off easily from the silpat mat when baked.

| | |
|---|---|
| **Sugar** | **250 g** |
| **Large eggs** | **4** |
| **Cocoa powder** | **10 g, sifted** |
| **Plain (all-purpose) flour** | **25 g, sifted** |
| **Orange** | **1/2, grated for zest** |
| **Almond flakes** | **250 g** |
| **Icing (confectioner's) sugar for dusting, sifted (optional)** | |

In a large bowl, beat together sugar and eggs. Add remaining ingredients, adding almonds last.

Line 2 baking trays with baking paper. Alternatively, line 1 baking tray and use a silpat mat over the other tray.

Preheat oven to 180°C.

Using a flat metal spatula, spread 7-cm tuile circles onto a lined baking tray or silpat mat.

Bake for 10–12 minutes until golden brown.

Once tray is out of the oven, quickly use a spatula to peel off tuiles and drape over a large rolling pin to shape. Gently remove shaped tuiles from rolling pin and place on a lined tray to set.

If remaining tuiles become hard before shaping, return tray to oven and heat for 1–2 minutes to soften them. Continue to shape tuiles until done.

Place set tuiles to cool on a wire rack, then store in an airtight container or refrigerator. Dust with icing sugar as desired when serving.

Makes 20 tuiles

# Chocolate Almond Caramel

A crunchy golden treat.

| | |
|---|---|
| **White almonds** | 150 g, whole or sliced |
| **Sugar** | 250 g |
| **Water** | 2 Tbsp |
| **Dark chocolate** | 100 g, chopped |

Line a baking tray with baking paper or use a silpat mat on a baking tray. Silpat mats are readily available from baking supplies shops.

Lightly toast almonds on prepared tray. Allow to cool on tray.

In a saucepan, caramelise sugar and water until golden brown, stirring continuously. Be careful not to burn syrup.

Pour over nuts in an even layer on tray. Let caramel set, then break using fingers or cut with a knife.

Melt dark chocolate in a bain-marie. Dip each caramel slice in melted chocolate.

Refrigerate or freeze for 1–2 hours before serving or using as a garnish with other desserts.

# Mousse

White Chocolate Mousse with Raspberry Coulis   *126*

Olive Chocolate Cream   *128*

Milk Chocolate Mousse Infused with Earl
Grey Tea and Passionfruit Sauce   *129*

# White Chocolate Mousse with Raspberry Coulis

*This is a rich mousse that has the right balance between sweet and sour.*

| | |
|---|---|
| **White chocolate** | **250 g, chopped** |
| **Butter** | **60 g, softened** |
| **Cream** | **400 ml** |
| **Raspberry coulis (see pg 139)** | |
| **Raspberries** | |

Prepare a bowl or 4–6 shot glasses.

Melt white chocolate and butter in a bain-marie.

Whip cream and fold into warm chocolate mixture.

Spoon mixture into bowl or shot glasses. Refrigerate for 2–3 hours.

Pipe raspberry coulis over chocolate mousse. Top with raspberries before serving.

Serves 4–6

## Olive Chocolate Cream

This versatile cream can be used with many desserts.

In a saucepan, bring cream, butter and corn syrup to a simmer over low heat.

Remove from heat and cool to 80°C. This is important as the sauce will curdle if the mixture is too hot.

Stir in dark chocolate and olive oil. Refrigerate for 1 hour.

Scoop chilled cream into quenelles or into small serving containers. Serve with a dessert of your choice.

Makes 6–8 servings

| | |
|---|---|
| Cream | 200 ml |
| Butter | 18 g |
| Light corn syrup | 50 ml |
| Dark chocolate | 200 g, chopped |
| Extra virgin olive oil | 20 ml |

# Milk Chocolate Mousse Infused with Earl Grey Tea and Passionfruit Sauce

This delicate and fragrant mousse is best eaten from small glasses.

**Fresh fruit**

**Assorted nuts**

*Mousse*

| | |
|---|---|
| **Sugar** | **100 g** |
| **Cream** | **300 ml** |
| **Milk** | **100 ml** |
| **Earl Grey tea** | **1 tea bag** |
| **Milk chocolate** | **250 g, chopped** |

*Passionfruit sauce*

| | |
|---|---|
| **Passionfruit** | **5** |
| **Water** | **60 ml** |
| **Sugar** | **60 g** |
| **Star anise** | **3** |

Prepare mousse. In a saucepan, bring sugar, cream and milk to a simmer over low heat.

Remove from heat and place tea bag into mixture. Cover and leave for 10 minutes.

Remove tea bag and pour mixture over milk chocolate. Stir well. Refrigerate for 2–3 hours.

Prepare passionfruit sauce. Scoop out passionfruit pulp into a saucepan. Add water, sugar and star anise. Bring to a simmer over low heat.

Smoothen sauce with a handheld blender for 20 seconds, then pass sauce through a sieve. Refrigerate for at least 1 hour.

Pour mousse into glasses and top with passionfruit sauce and your choice of fresh fruit and/or nuts before serving.

Serves 6–8

*Photo on pg 130*

# Basic Recipes and Tips

# Chocolate Ganache

This ganache can be used with both cakes and biscuits.

| | |
|---|---|
| **Cream** | **100 ml** |
| **Dark chocolate** | **180 g, chopped** |

In a saucepan, heat cream. Once bubbles appear, remove from heat and stir in chocolate. Allow to cool.

Refrigerate for 10–15 minutes before using.

# Chocolate Mayonnaise

An unusually delicious and creamy sauce.

| | |
|---|---|
| **Milk chocolate** | **250 g, chopped** |
| **Egg yolks** | **6** |
| **Sugar** | **250 g** |
| **Salt** | **a pinch** |
| **Butter** | **150 g, softened** |
| **Egg whites** | **14** |

Melt chocolate in a bain-marie.

In a mixing bowl, whisk egg yolks, sugar and salt together, then add butter.

Fold in melted chocolate, then refrigerate for 1 hour.

In another mixing bowl, beat egg whites until stiff peaks form. Fold into chilled mixture.

Store in an airtight container and keep refrigerated. Use with any dessert recipe.

# Chocolate Ice Cream

You'll need an ice cream maker for this classic favourite.

| | |
|---|---|
| **Milk** | **500 ml** |
| **Cream** | **100 ml** |
| **Water** | **50 ml** |
| **Dark chocolate** | **250 g, chopped** |
| **Cocoa powder** | **40 g** |
| **Egg yolks** | **5** |
| **Sugar** | **150 g** |
| **Mocha sauce**<br>    **(optional)**<br>    **(see pg 139)** | |
| **Chocolate glaze**<br>    **(optional)**<br>    **(see pg 140)** | |

In a saucepan, bring milk, cream and water to the boil. Stir in dark chocolate and cocoa powder.

In a mixing bowl, beat egg yolks and sugar. Stir in some warm milk mixture to temper egg yolks.

Pour tempered mixture back into saucepan and mix well with remaining milk mixture.

Heat to 85°C, stirring constantly with a wooden spoon. It is important to monitor the temperature as the mixture will curdle if it gets too hot.

Transfer to a bowl and leave to cool to room temperature. Cover with plastic wrap such that  wrap touches the surface of cream. Refrigerate for at least 3 hours, until cold.

Transfer to an ice cream maker and churn according to the manufacturer's instructions.

Serve drizzled with mocha sauce or chocolate glaze as desired.

Makes 1 litre

# Raspberry Coulis

This is another basic recipe which can be used with many other dessert recipes.

| | |
|---|---|
| **Raspberries** | 500 g |
| **Sugar** | 60 g |

In a saucepan, cook raspberries and sugar until juices run and raspberries are soft.

Blend (process) with a handheld blender and pass coulis through a sieve if desired.

Refrigerate until ready to use.

# Mocha Sauce

This is a highly versatile basic sauce.

| | |
|---|---|
| **Sugar** | 100 g |
| **Coffee** | 135 ml |
| **Cream** | 50 ml |
| **Dark chocolate** | 50 g, chopped |

In a saucepan, combine all ingredients and bring to the boil, stirring. Allow to cool before using with dessert recipes.

# Chocolate Glaze

A beautiful glaze that is shiny and satiny when poured over desserts.

| | |
|---|---|
| **Dark chocolate** | **200 g, chopped** |
| **Unsalted butter** | **140 g, softened** |
| **Unsweetened cocoa powder** | **40 g** |
| Light corn syrup | 224 ml |

Melt dark chocolate in a bain-marie.

Transfer to a saucepan and add butter, cocoa powder and corn syrup. Stir well to mix.

Bring to the boil and remove from heat. Leave to cool at room temperature before using with other recipes.

# Pastry Cream

This is a basic cream which can be used in many dessert recipes.

| | |
|---|---|
| **Milk** | **500 ml** |
| **Whole vanilla bean** | **1, scraped for seeds and reserve pod, or 1 tsp vanilla essence** |
| **Large eggs** | **2** |
| **Sugar** | **100 g** |
| **Corn flour (cornstarch)** | **25 g** |
| **Butter** | **50 g, softened** |

In a saucepan, bring milk to the boil with vanilla seeds and pod.

In a mixing bowl, beat eggs, sugar and corn flour. Stir in some warm milk mixture.

Pour mixture back into saucepan and bring to the boil, stirring constantly with a whisk. The mixture will thicken and bubble. Remove from heat and whisk in butter.

Transfer mixture onto a flat tray and cover with plastic wrap such that wrap touches the surface of cream.

Refrigerate for at least 30 minutes or until ready to use. Use straight from tray or transfer to a mixing bowl and stir to soften slightly before using.

# Melting and Tempering Chocolate

## Melting chocolate

Before tempering, the chocolate must be melted. The ideal melting temperature is 40°–45°C. You can melt the chocolate at higher temperatures, but you must take care not to burn it, especially when using milk chocolate and white chocolate.

A good way to melt chocolate is to place it in a bowl set over a heated water bath or what is known as a bain-marie. The water level in the water bath should be low so that moisture or steam does not get into the chocolate. If water comes into contact with the chocolate, the quality of the chocolate will be affected.

Another way is to melt the chocolate in the microwave oven on Low. Keep the chocolate in the microwave oven for only 2–3 minutes at a time, and remove to stir at regular intervals so that it does not burn.

## Tempering chocolate

Tempering is simply bringing the chocolate to the working temperature. This gives chocolate, especially dark chocolate, a good gloss. It helps the chocolate to contract and unmould easily. Tempered chocolate has a good snap because it has a good crystal structure.

To temper chocolate well, you have to:

- Keep an eye on the temperature

- Allow time for the chocolate to reach the right temperature

- Stir the chocolate so that the crystals in the chocolate will align correctly

This involves the following steps:

- Melt the chocolate to 40°–45°C

- Cool the chocolate to about 32°C over an ice bath (a bowl set over ice and water in a large bowl)

- Re-heat the chocolate to about 35°C

And remember, while tempering chocolate, keep stirring it constantly.

*Tip:* When tempering chocolate, a shortcut method is to melt the chocolate, then add additional fine shavings or small pieces of chocolate to cool the melted chocolate mass, while stirring all the time. Leave the chocolate to rest a short while, then stir again.

# Weights and Measures

Quantities for this book are given in Metric and American (spoon and cup) measures. Standard spoon and cup measurements used are: 1 tsp = 5 ml, 1 Tbsp = 15 ml, 1 cup = 250 ml. All measures are level unless otherwise stated.

## LIQUID AND VOLUME MEASURES

| Metric | Imperial | American |
|---|---|---|
| 5 ml | $^1/_6$ fl oz | 1 teaspoon |
| 10 ml | $^1/_3$ fl oz | 1 dessertspoon |
| 15 ml | $^1/_2$ fl oz | 1 tablespoon |
| 60 ml | 2 fl oz | $^1/_4$ cup (4 tablespoons) |
| 85 ml | $2^1/_2$ fl oz | $^1/_3$ cup |
| 90 ml | 3 fl oz | $^3/_8$ cup (6 tablespoons) |
| 125 ml | 4 fl oz | $^1/_2$ cup |
| 180 ml | 6 fl oz | $^3/_4$ cup |
| 250 ml | 8 fl oz | 1 cup |
| 300 ml | 10 fl oz ($^1/_2$ pint) | $1^1/_4$ cups |
| 375 ml | 12 fl oz | $1^1/_2$ cups |
| 435 ml | 14 fl oz | $1^3/_4$ cups |
| 500 ml | 16 fl oz | 2 cups |
| 625 ml | 20 fl oz (1 pint) | $2^1/_2$ cups |
| 750 ml | 24 fl oz ($1^1/_5$ pints) | 3 cups |
| 1 litre | 32 fl oz ($1^3/_5$ pints) | 4 cups |
| 1.25 litres | 40 fl oz (2 pints) | 5 cups |
| 1.5 litres | 48 fl oz ($2^2/_5$ pints) | 6 cups |
| 2.5 litres | 80 fl oz (4 pints) | 10 cups |

## DRY MEASURES

| Metric | Imperial |
|---|---|
| 30 grams | 1 ounce |
| 45 grams | $1^1/_2$ ounces |
| 55 grams | 2 ounces |
| 70 grams | $2^1/_2$ ounces |
| 85 grams | 3 ounces |
| 100 grams | $3^1/_2$ ounces |
| 110 grams | 4 ounces |
| 125 grams | $4^1/_2$ ounces |
| 140 grams | 5 ounces |
| 280 grams | 10 ounces |
| 450 grams | 16 ounces (1 pound) |
| 500 grams | 1 pound, $1^1/_2$ ounces |
| 700 grams | $1^1/_2$ pounds |
| 800 grams | $1^3/_4$ pounds |
| 1 kilogram | 2 pounds, 3 ounces |
| 1.5 kilograms | 3 pounds, $4^1/_2$ ounces |
| 2 kilograms | 4 pounds, 6 ounces |

## LENGTH

| Metric | Imperial |
|---|---|
| 0.5 cm | $^1/_4$ inch |
| 1 cm | $^1/_2$ inch |
| 1.5 cm | $^3/_4$ inch |
| 2.5 cm | 1 inch |

## OVEN TEMPERATURE

| | °C | °F | Gas Regulo |
|---|---|---|---|
| Very slow | 120 | 250 | 1 |
| Slow | 150 | 300 | 2 |
| Moderately slow | 160 | 325 | 3 |
| Moderate | 180 | 350 | 4 |
| Moderately hot | 190/200 | 370/400 | 5/6 |
| Hot | 210/220 | 410/440 | 6/7 |
| Very hot | 230 | 450 | 8 |
| Super hot | 250/290 | 475/550 | 9/10 |

## ABBREVIATION

| | |
|---|---|
| tsp | teaspoon |
| Tbsp | tablespoon |
| g | gram |
| kg | kilogram |
| ml | millilitre |